HEATH ROBINSON

On Travel

AMBERLEY

First published 2015

Amberley Publishing
The Hill, Stroud
Gloucestershire, GL5 4EP

www.amberley-books.com

British Library Cataloguing in Publication Data.
A catalogue record for this book is available from the British Library.

ISBN 978 1 4456 4595 7 (paperback)
ISBN 978 1 4456 4601 5 (ebook)

Typesetting and Origination by Amberley Publishing.
Printed in the UK.

Contents

Introduction

Most of us are certain we could improve Britain's transport system if only we put a little bit of thought into it. However, it is a sad fact of life that, no matter how sensible and revolutionary our ideas may be, to introduce major changes would be extremely difficult and would inevitably be crushed by a bewildering amount of paperwork.

Luckily, though, help is at hand. Through the drawings of William Heath Robinson, we can avoid all such stressful processes and see these brilliant ideas brought to life on the page far, far sooner than we would ever be able to see them in reality. Having lived through an age that saw travel redefined in terms of comfort, speed and technology, and having witnessed the dramatic expansion of our world as global travel became available for more and more people, Heath Robinson is perfectly poised to offer his expertise.

Our railway system, always a source of frustration for the weary commuter, is re-imagined with great skill, from crowded carriages to the methods of construction used for various railway bridges. We also gain a valuable insight into the hidden world of the railway employee, exploring both peculiar training techniques and the varied duties they undertake.

Nor is the common motorist forgotten. Travel by road may have been in its relative infancy during Heath Robinson's lifetime, but this in no way means that the modern road user – by bus, car, bicycle or even on foot – cannot find common ground within, from the chaos caused by snow to the many perils of caravanning. Heath Robinson's inventions provide the logical answer to many common problems we may not have realised existed; why drive around a chicken on the road, for example, when you can simply hop over it?

Finally, mankind's forays into the world's oceans (and ponds) and the skies above us are fully explored, from zeppelin to fishing boat, from wartime antics to an insight into the world of leisure cruises.

Altogether, then, this remarkable collection expresses in many ways the long-abandoned aspirations of a nation disgruntled by its own failure to get anywhere on time. It is the ideal book to read on a train, on a bus, on a plane – or while waiting for any of those to arrive. It will surely send budding transport engineers scrambling for their pencils, while providing existing transport engineers with, at the very least, a smile to brighten their disillusioned lives.

1
By Rail

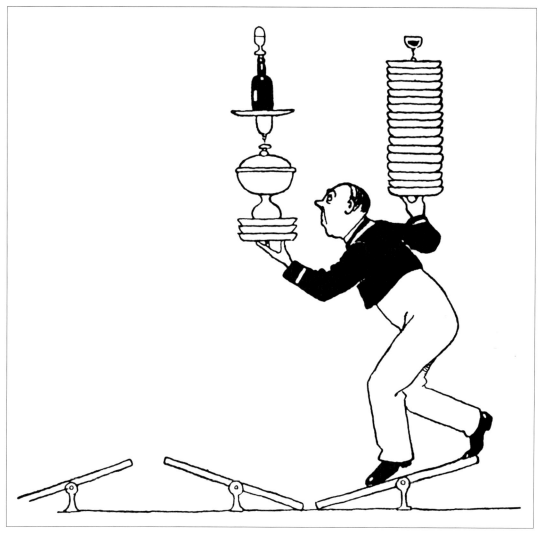

Training restaurant car attendant to carry on during uncertain motion of train.

How the trains get delayed on the London, Brighton and South Coast Railway. Nothing of this sort happened when the volunteers ran the trains during the strike.

Our sixth column frustrates a dastardly attempt by the fifth to tamper with a railway signal.

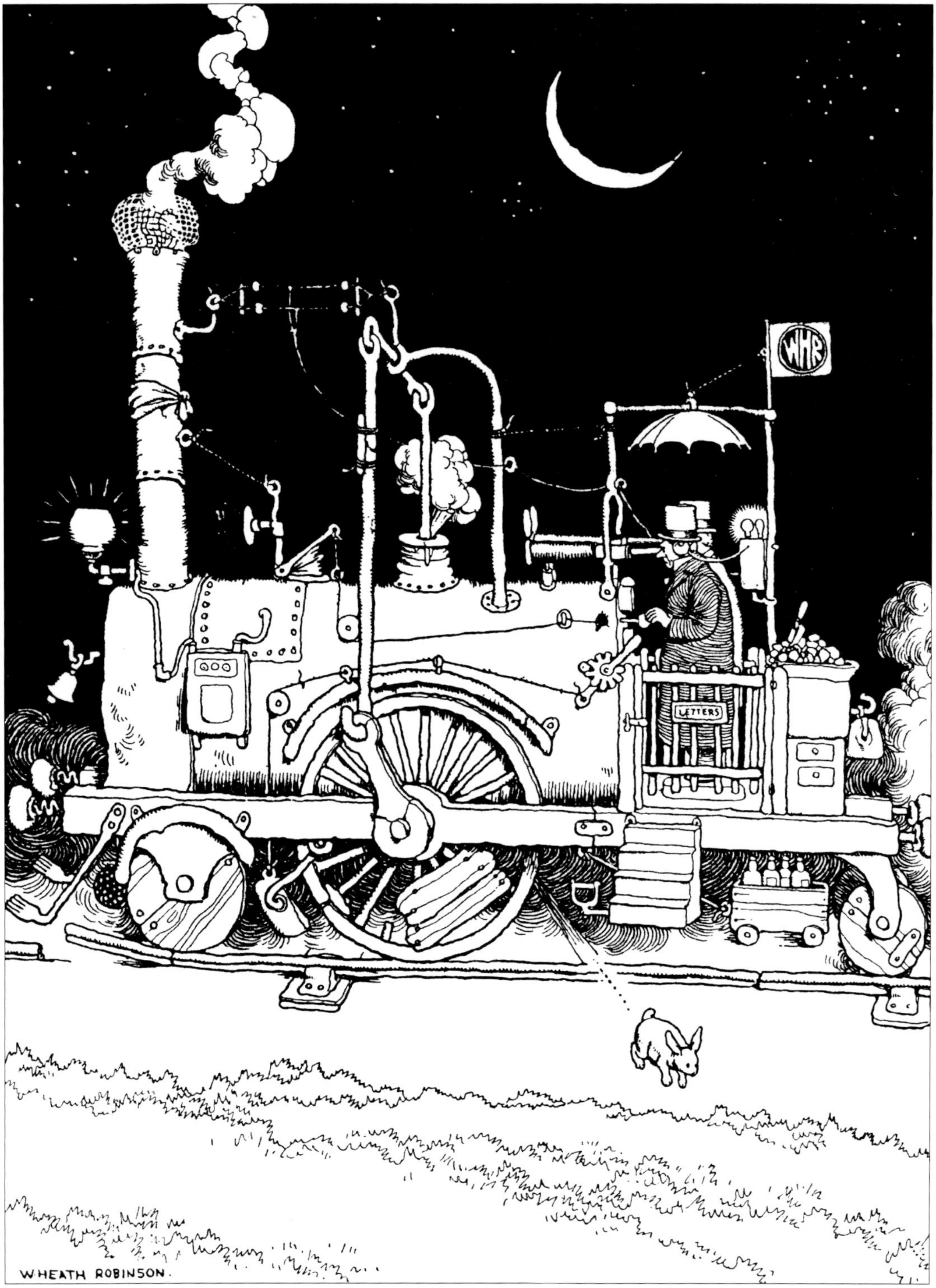
WHR
LETTERS
W. HEATH ROBINSON.

Mr W. Heath Robinson's own private railway engine, not often allowed on the GWR.

Building the first locomotive.

Night duty at one of the first railway signals.

Goods and passengers carried together in the open.

Pulling the communication cord in one of the old open carriages.

A very early type of mechanical signal, now rarely to be seen!

The first excursion train.

The first 'ladies only' compartment.

The building of Saltash Bridge.

The first smoking carriage.

The first bathing compartment.

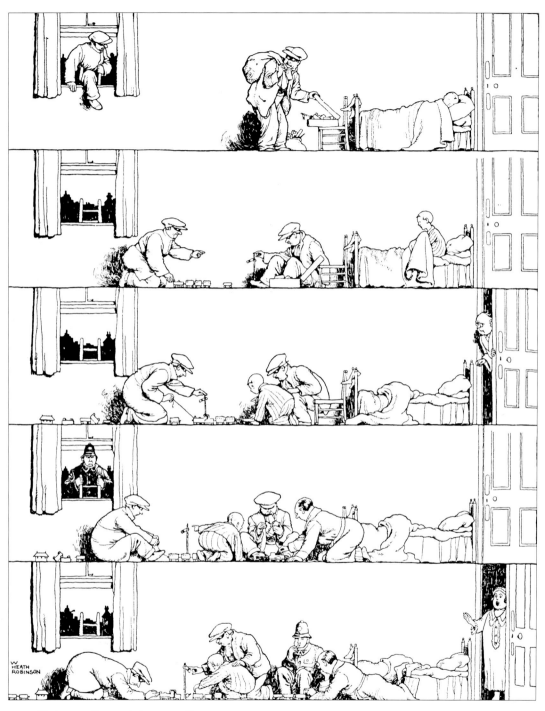

Christmas Eve and the toy railway.

Taking seats for lunch on one of the first trains to be equipped with restaurant cars.

How they negotiated the flooded districts in the short cut to the west.

One of the many suggestions for doing without tunnels.

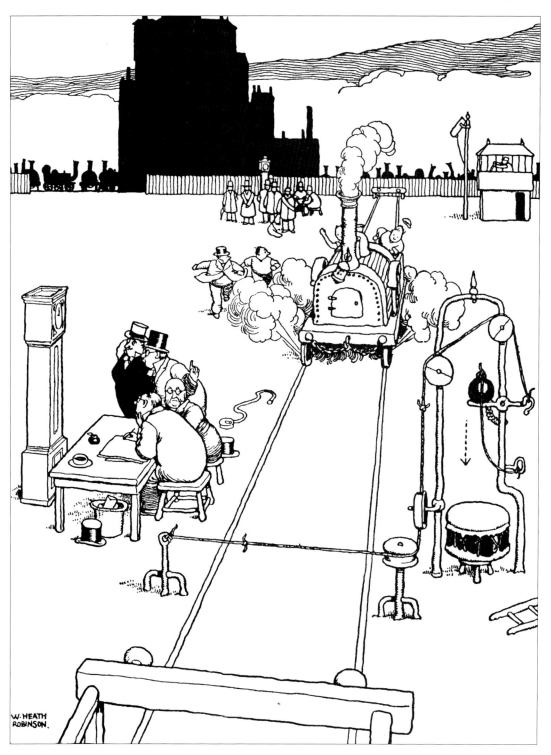

An old-fashioned method of testing the speed of engines.

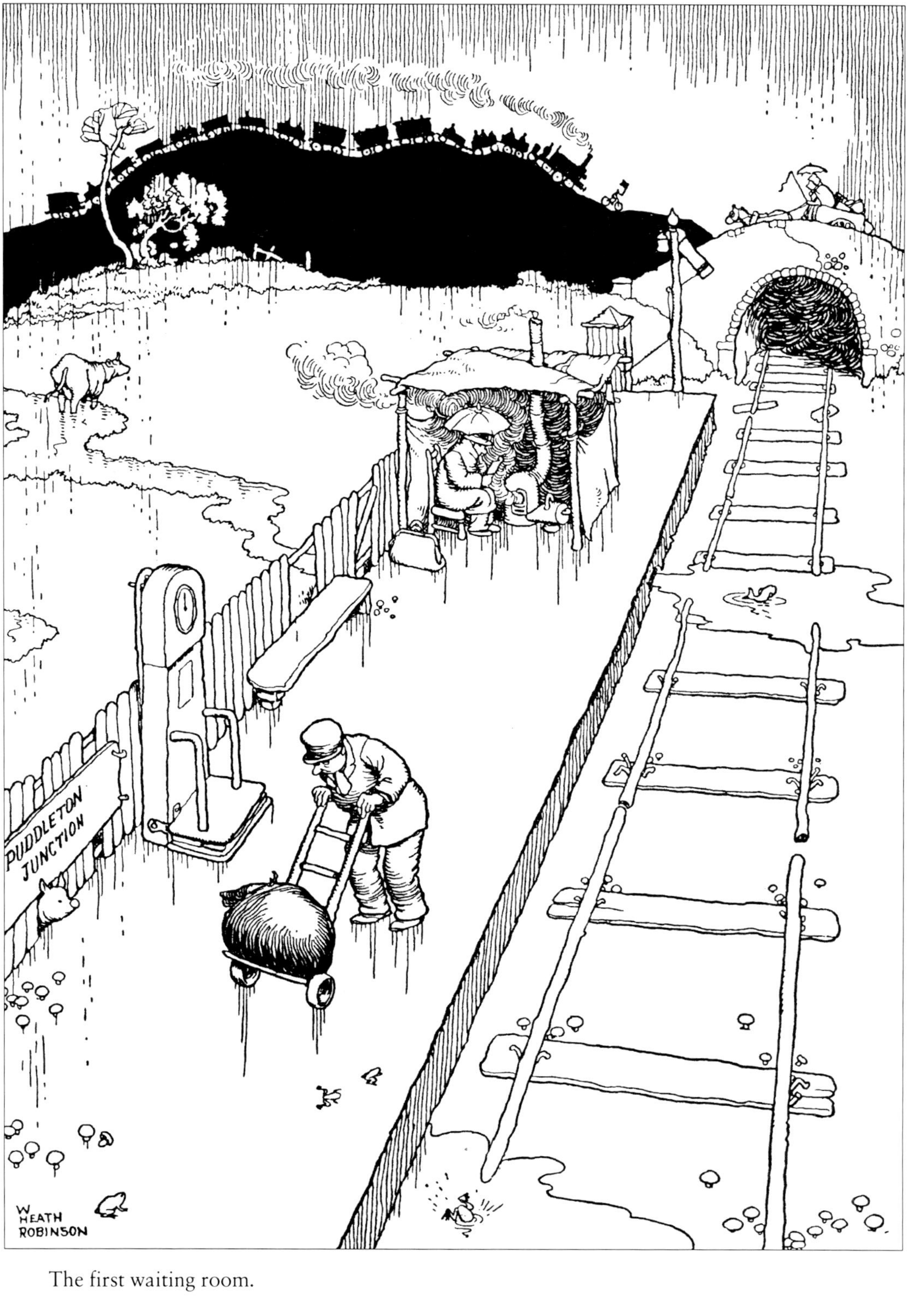
PUDDLETON JUNCTION
W HEATH ROBINSON

The first waiting room.

A picturesque ceremony – the mayor in state letting through the first train in a new railway station.

An antiquated method of filling the boilers without stopping the engine before the introduction of the water-trough system.

An early type of engine for cleaning tunnels.

The change over from broad gauge to narrow gauge.

Checking the first timetable before publication.

Varied duties of railway police.

Sectional view of the excavations for the Severn Tunnel, showing the hard and fossiliferous nature of the ground to be penetrated.

How they teach young engine drivers the meaning of signals.

A well-thought-out and nearly successful experiment by early railway pioneer.

TRAINING MEMBERS OF THE STAFF TO CLOSE
THE CARRIAGE DOORS WHEN THE TRAIN IS IN MOTION

TRAINING TICKET COLLECTORS

W. HEATH ROBINSON

Traning the staff.

Relieving the tedium of waiting for the signal on the slow train – between Paddington and Land's End via Southampton, Hereford and Weston-super-Mare.

The new humane cow-catcher.

2

By Road

Testing a new type of steering gear.

Very hot! The wonderful Heath Robinson new patent thawing machine. This stupendous invention has been specially designed to enable the pedestrian to walk with confidence on the most slippery roads.

The Kinecar: an ingenious vehicle fitted with many devices for the comfort and amusement of passengers returning on winter evenings.

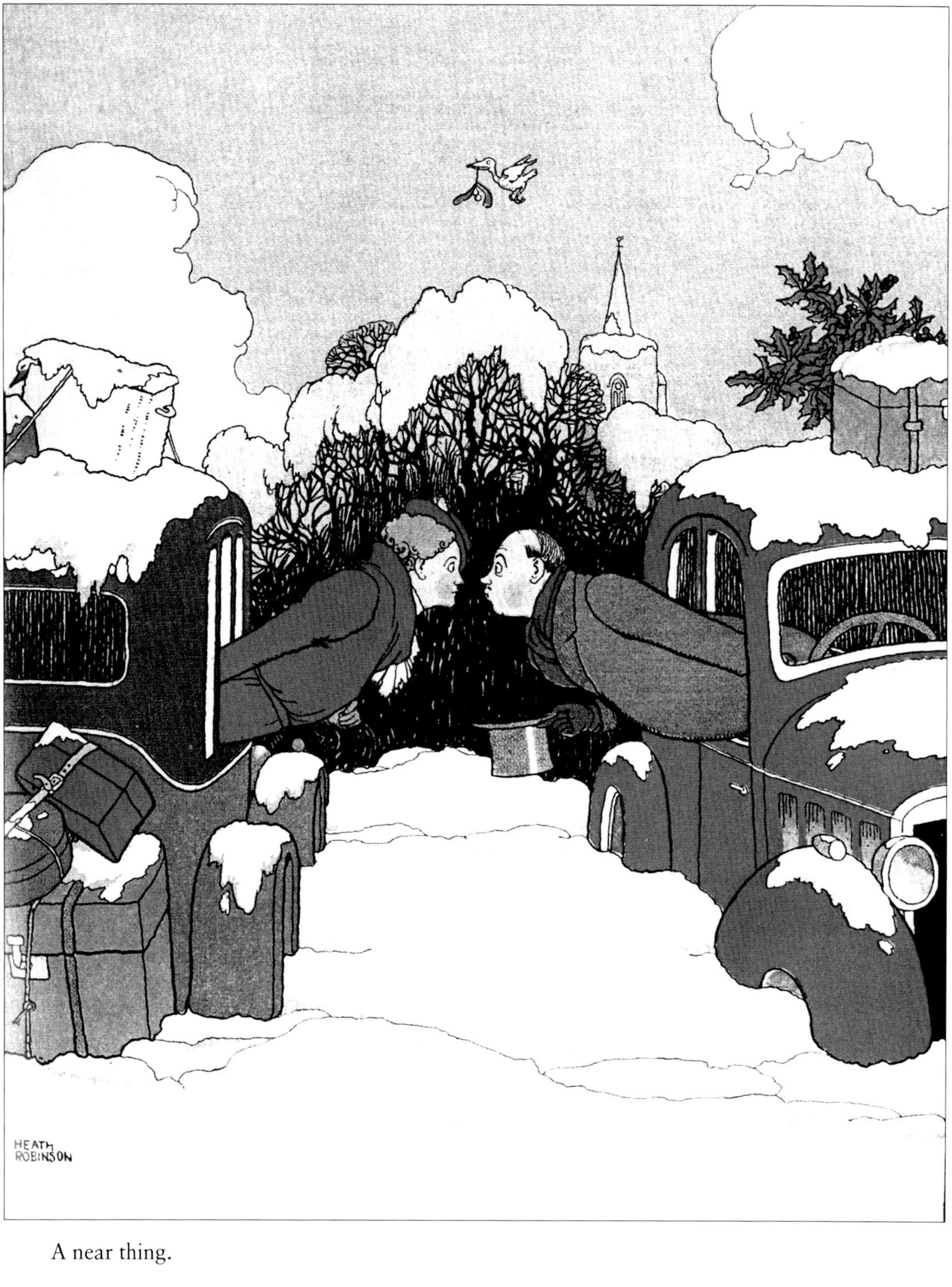
HEATH
ROBINSON

A near thing.

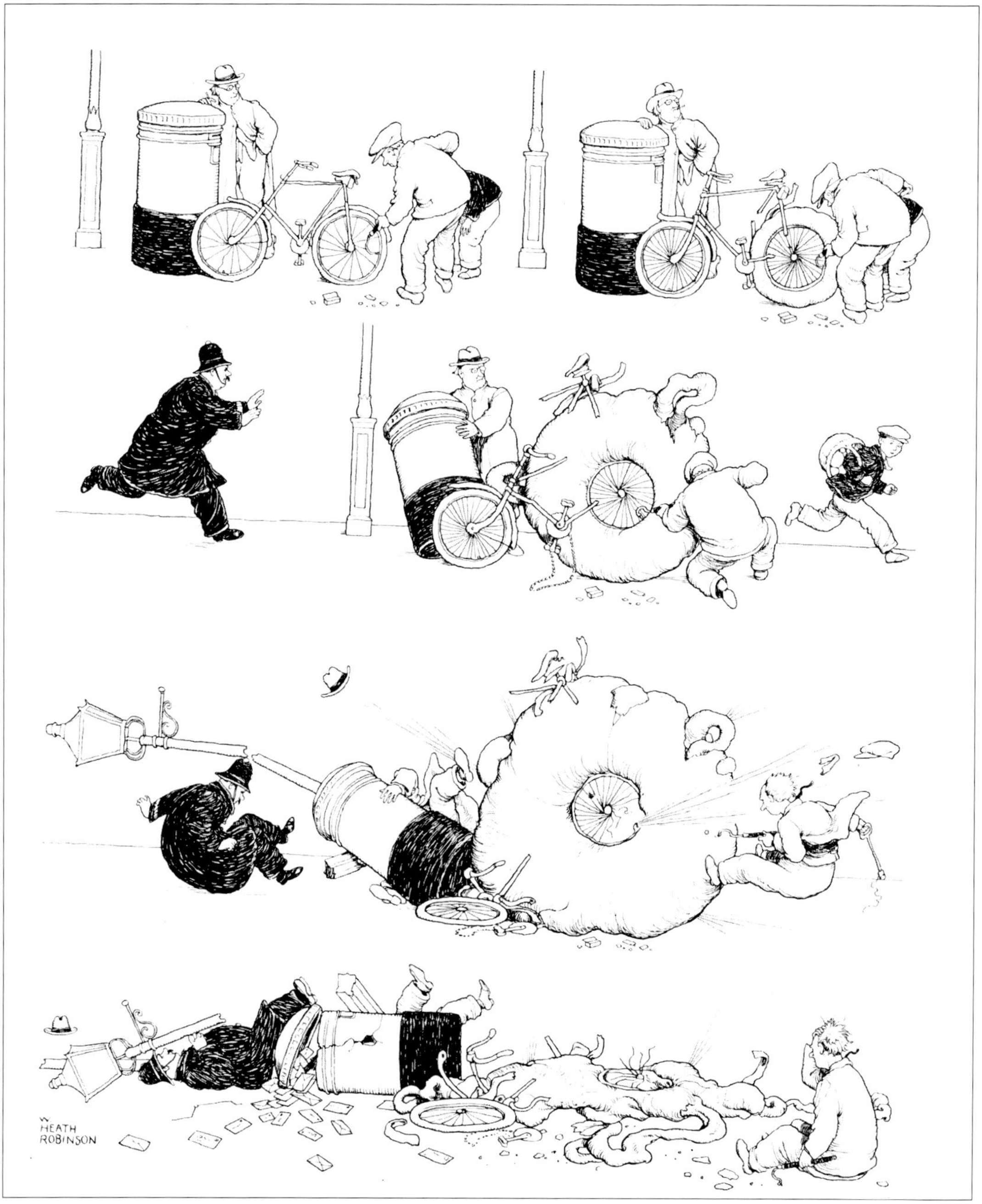
W HEATH ROBINSON

The puncture.

The new safety-fork adjustment for motor-cars for the protection of chickens on the road.

One-at-a-time lock in Brompton Road.

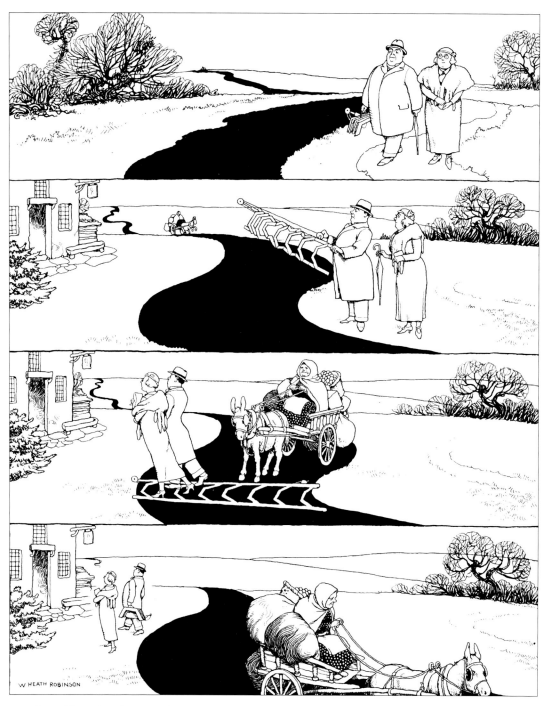

Portable pedestrian crossings.

The war lord at the front: a morning tub on the imperial campaigning car.

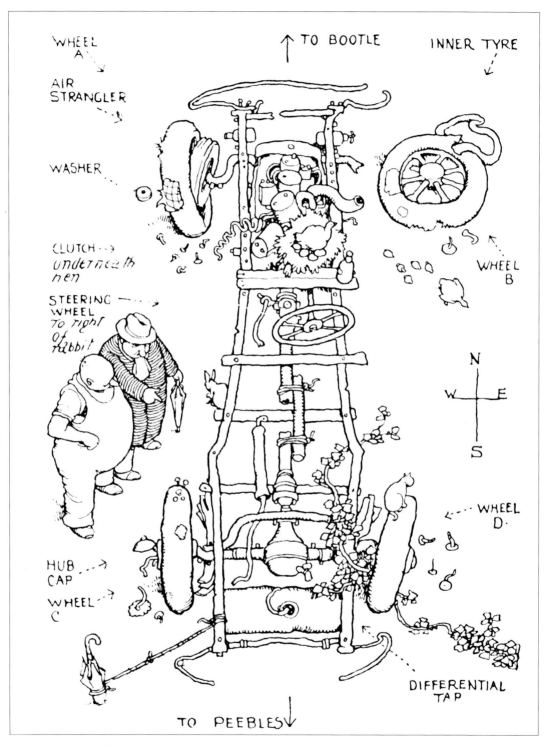

Explanatory diagram of a typical modern chassis.

Judging artistic effect before purchase.

Choosing a car to match your wife's compexion.

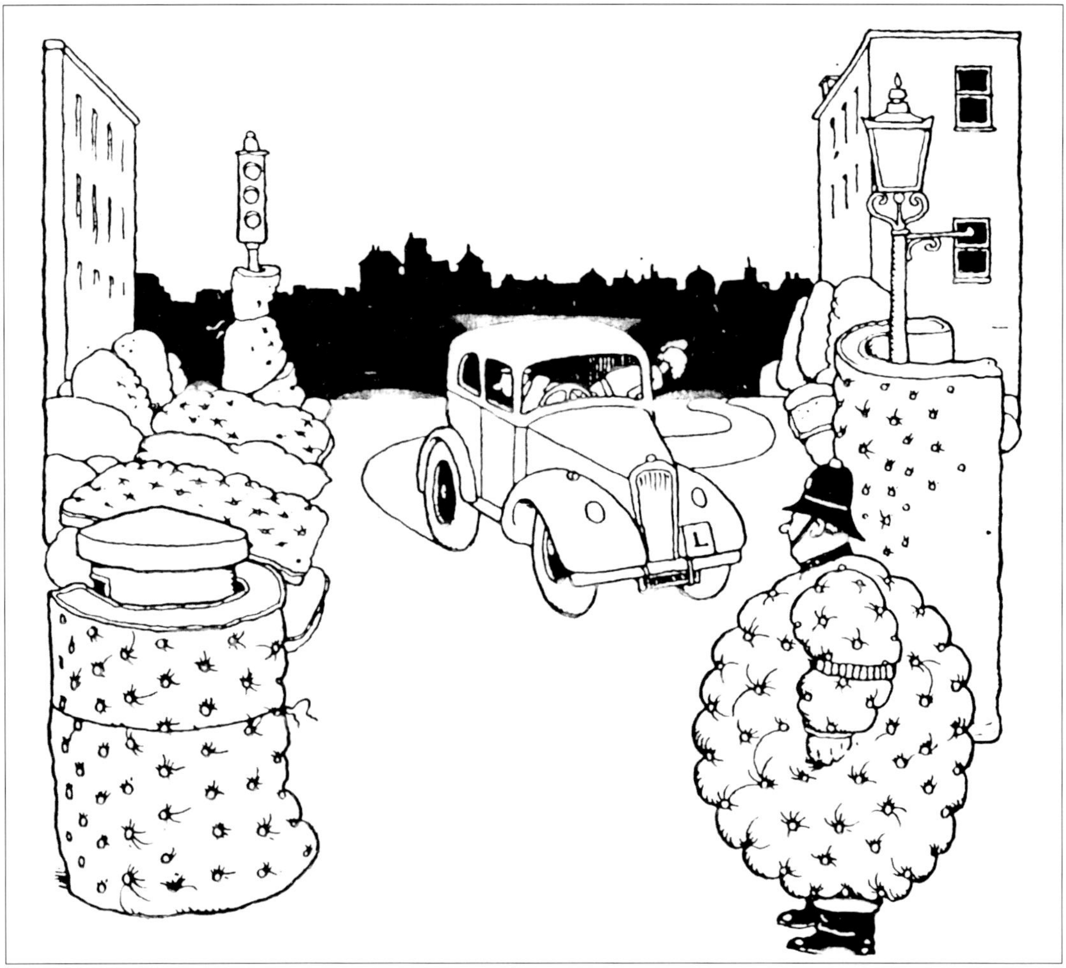
L

The new safety street for learners.

Teaching the meaning of hand signals made by the car in front.

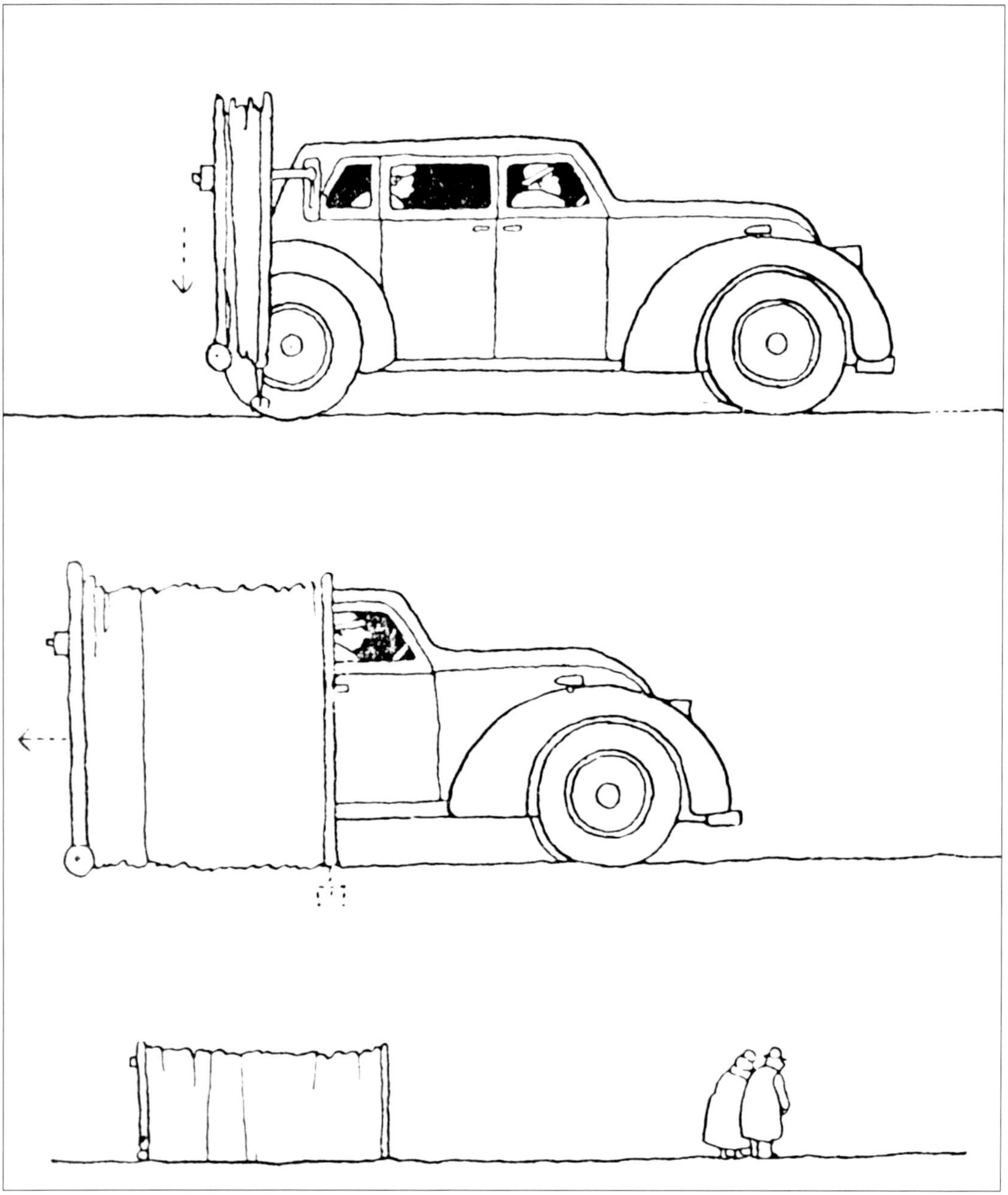

The portable garage.

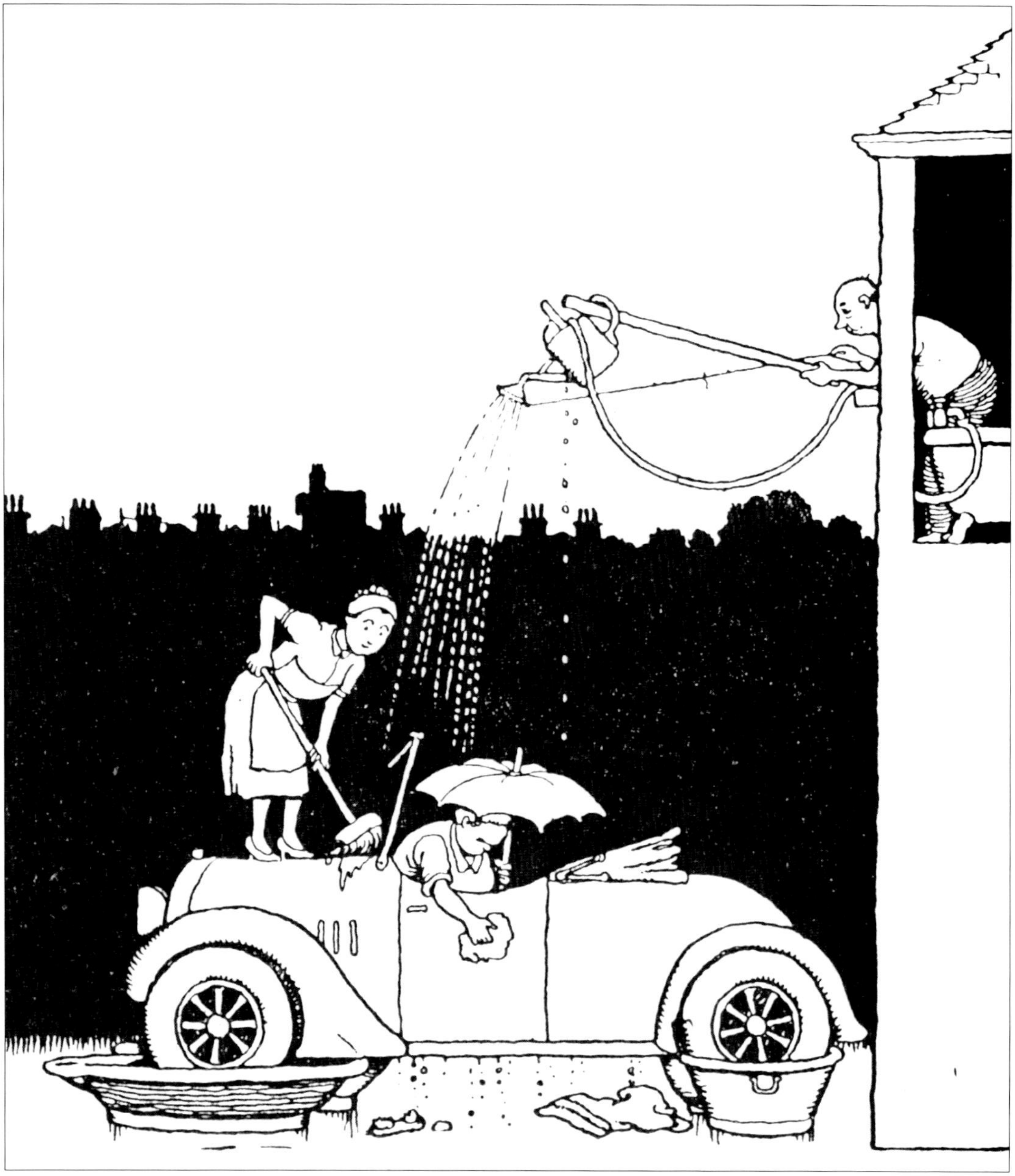

Cleaning the car.

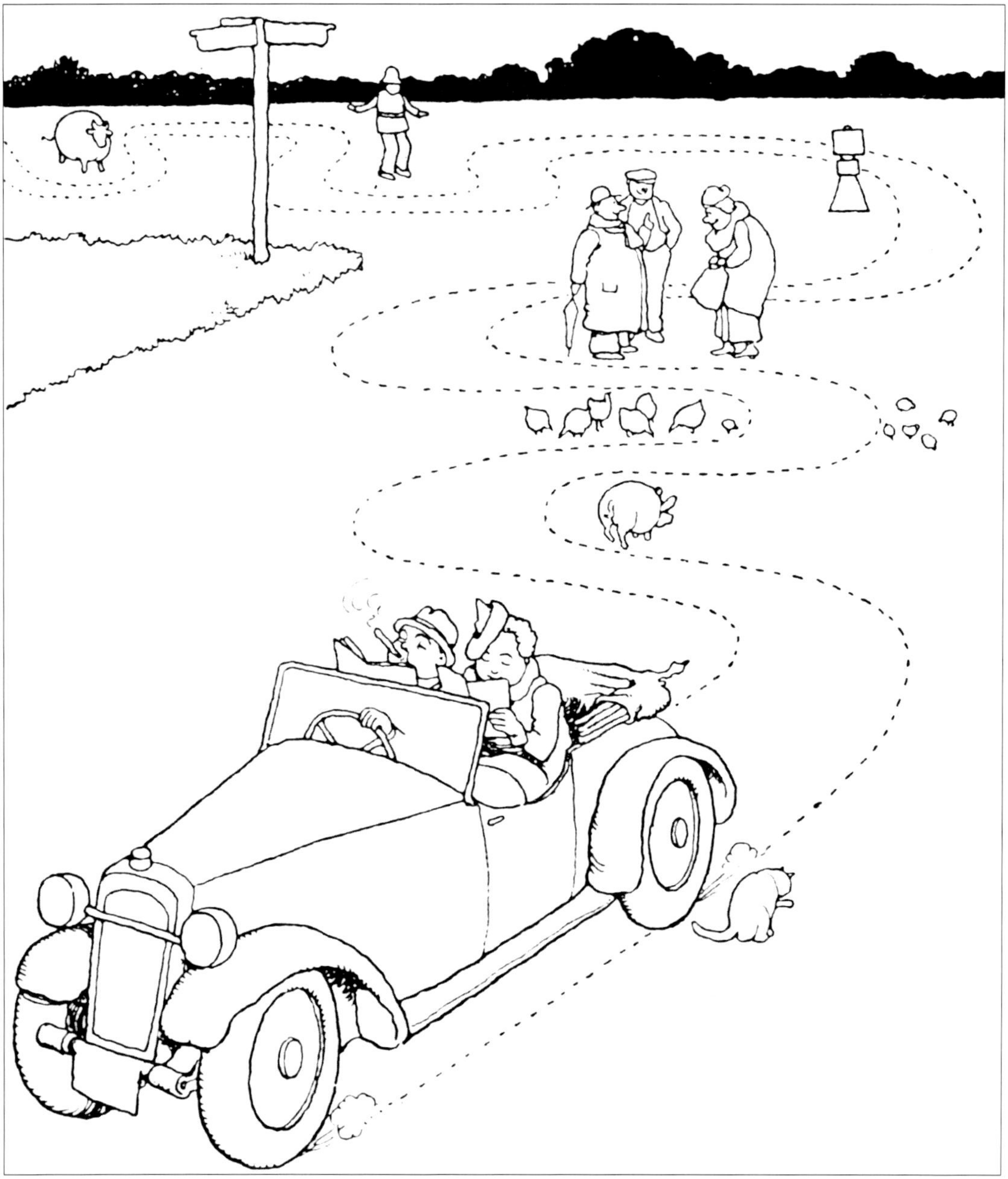

Road sense.

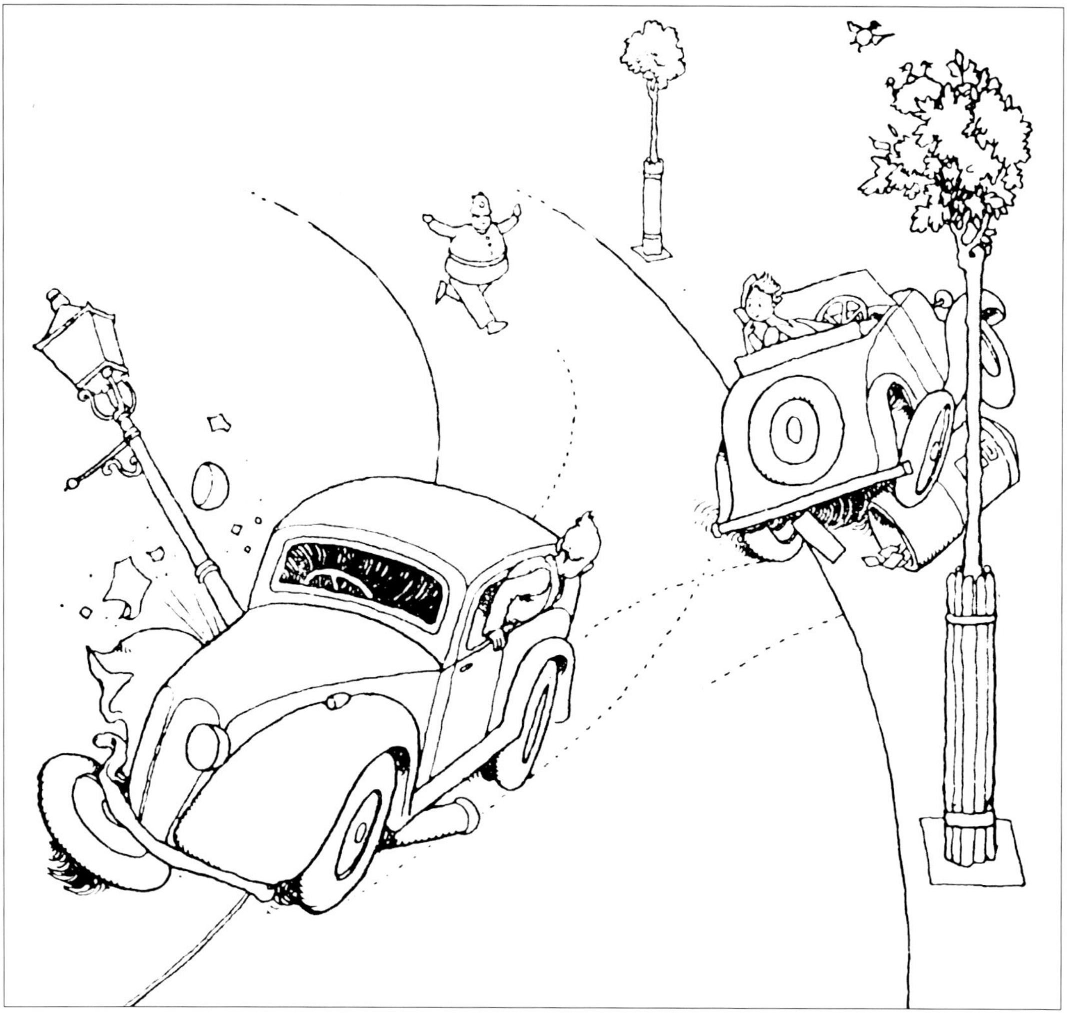

Love at first sight.

Deciding the right of way.

The modesty bathing car.

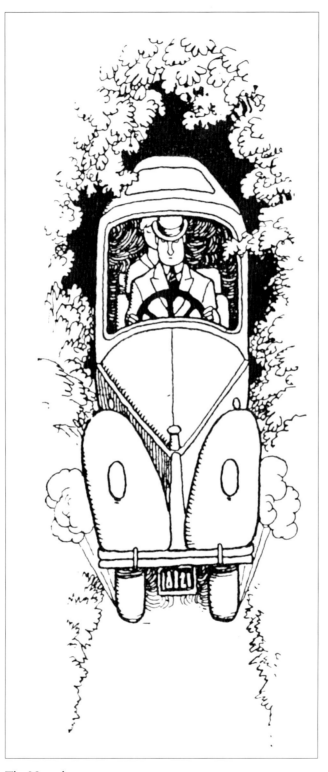

The Narrokar.

The sideways body for the discomfiture of road hogs.

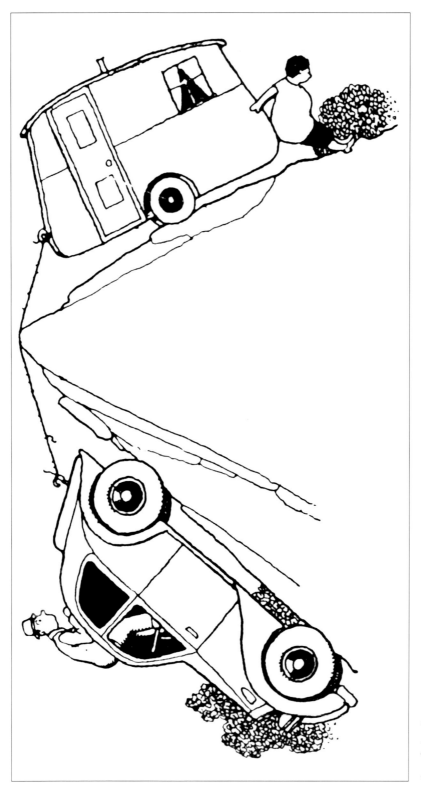

An alpine impasse.

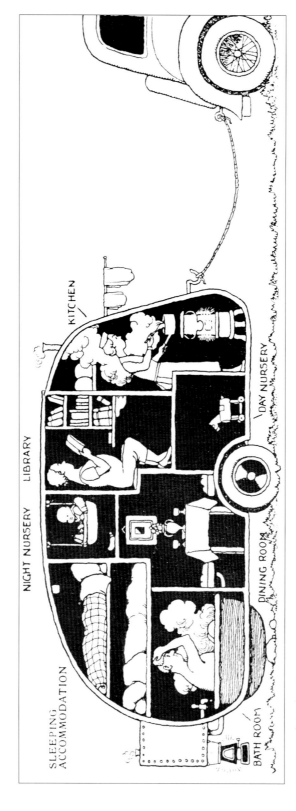

Interior of the family caravan.

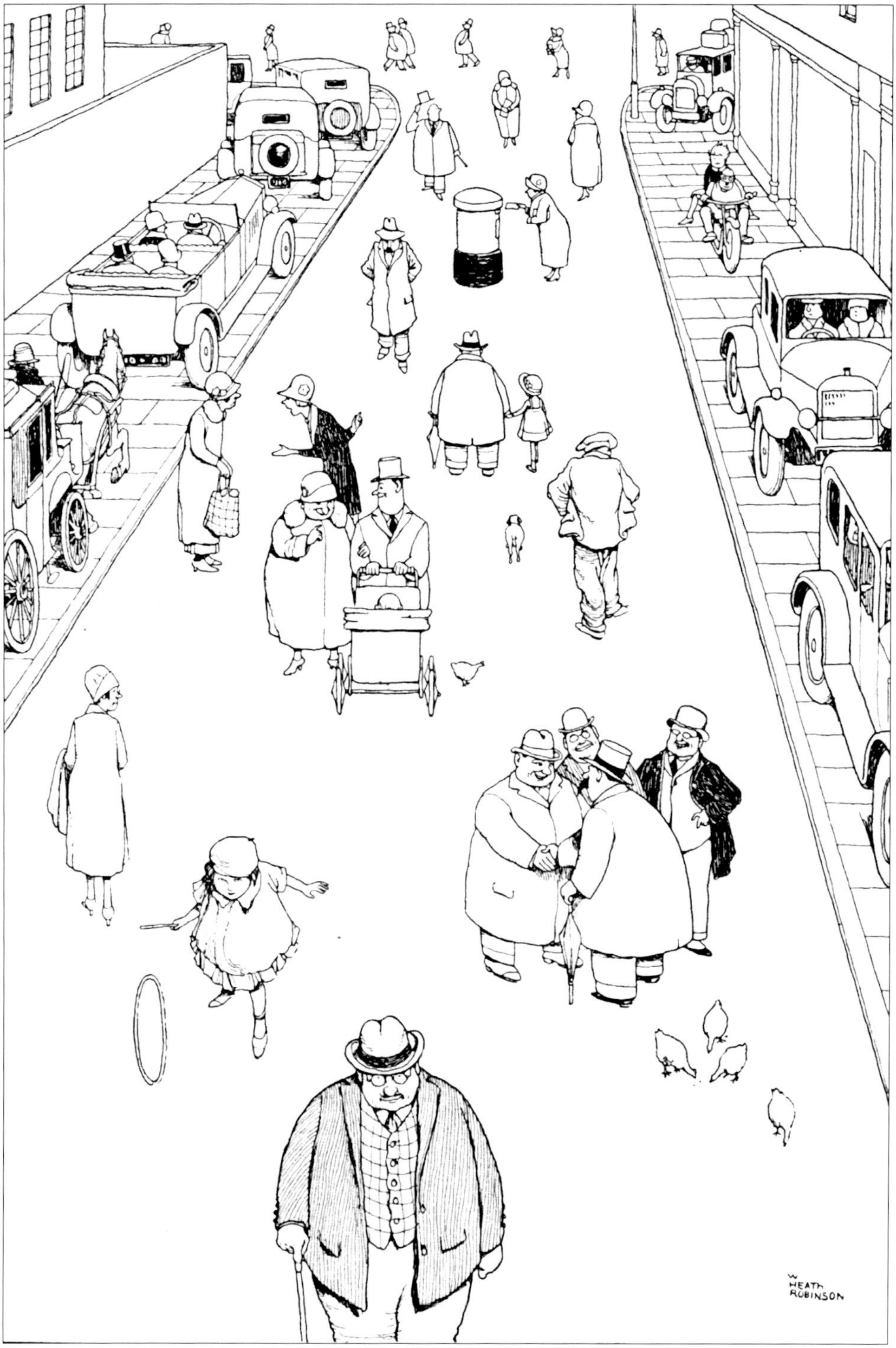
W HEATH ROBINSON

Safety first! New road regulations shortly to be introduced to ensure the safety and comfort of pedestrians.

An awkward predicament.

A new snow-plough for clearing a footpath after a heavy fall.

Elasticity: disinterested conduct of kind-hearted motorists to sufferers from the bad state of the roads.

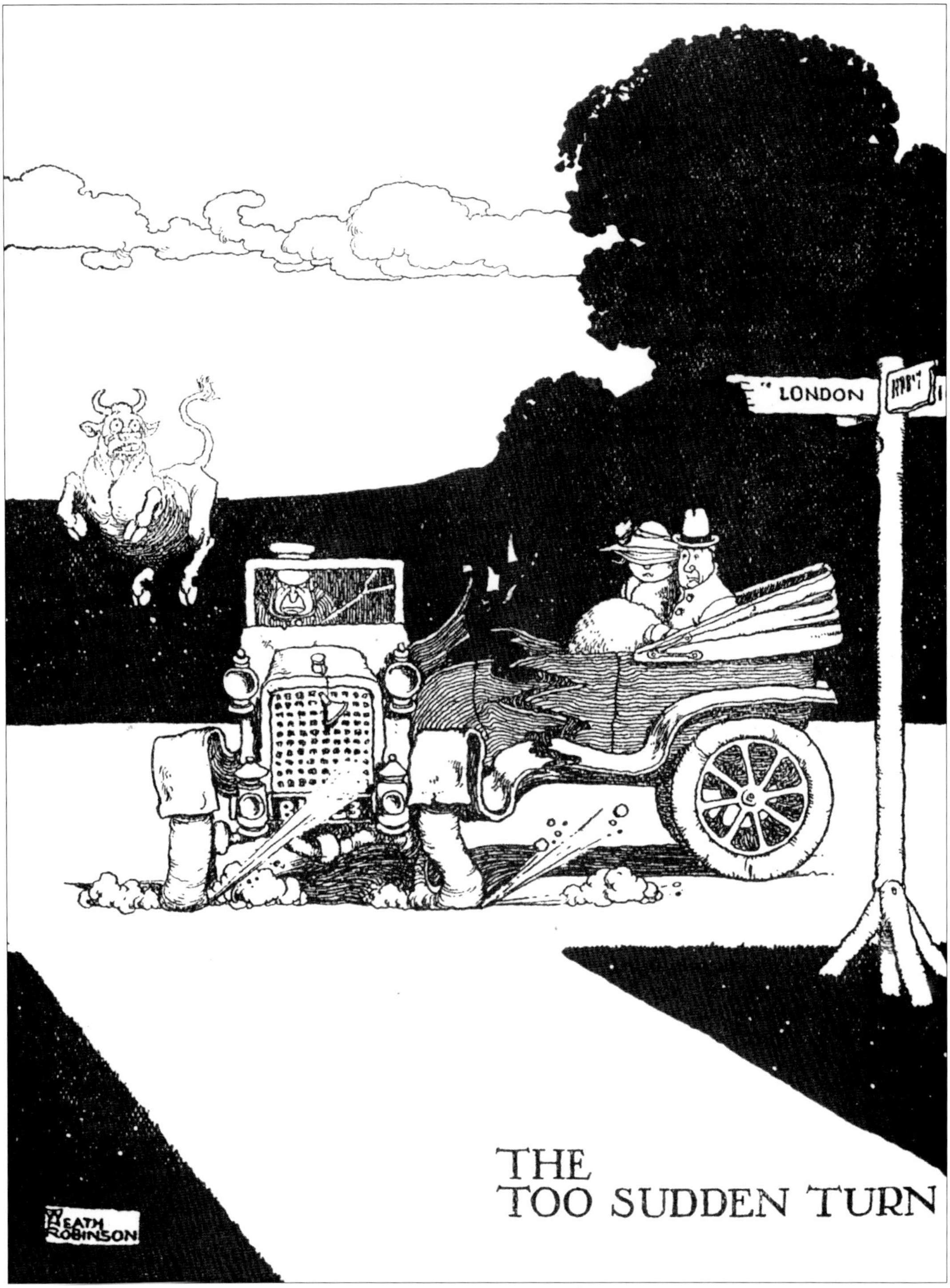
LONDON
THE
TOO SUDDEN TURN
HEATH
ROBINSON

The too-sudden turn.

Subsidence on the Brighton road.

3

By Sea and Sky

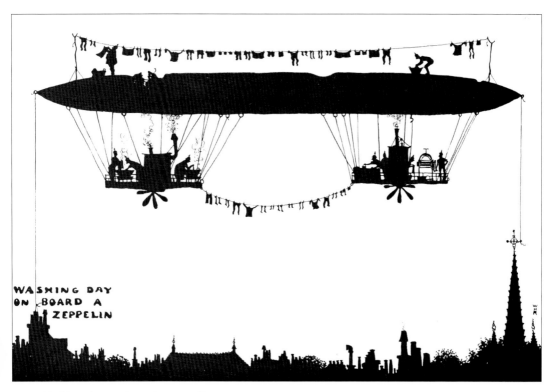

Washing day on board a zeppelin.

OH U! The German periscoper: 'Ach Himmel! Dot most be der peautiful Ben Nevis of vich ve 'ave 'eard so mooch!'

Spiked! Unfortunate mishap to a Zeppelin through a lack of proper caution in descending.

The hydro-multi-aeroplane.

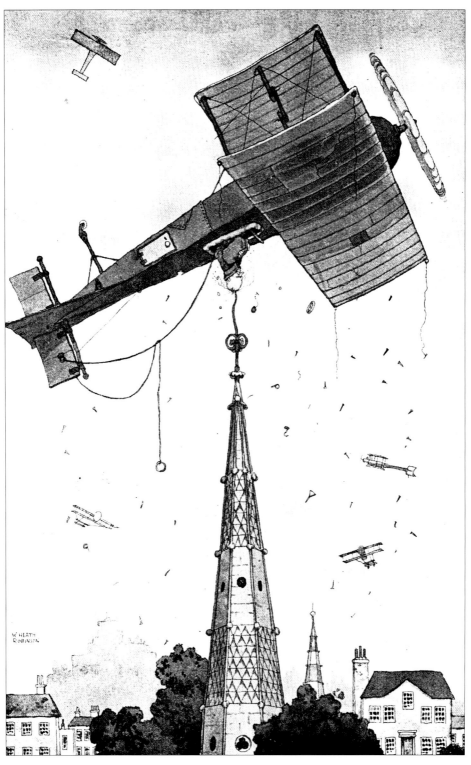

An aeronaut scratching his head over a difficult problem.

An imperial measure: the cunning contrivance of a denizen of Sheppey conveying his family to mainland en route for Wembley.

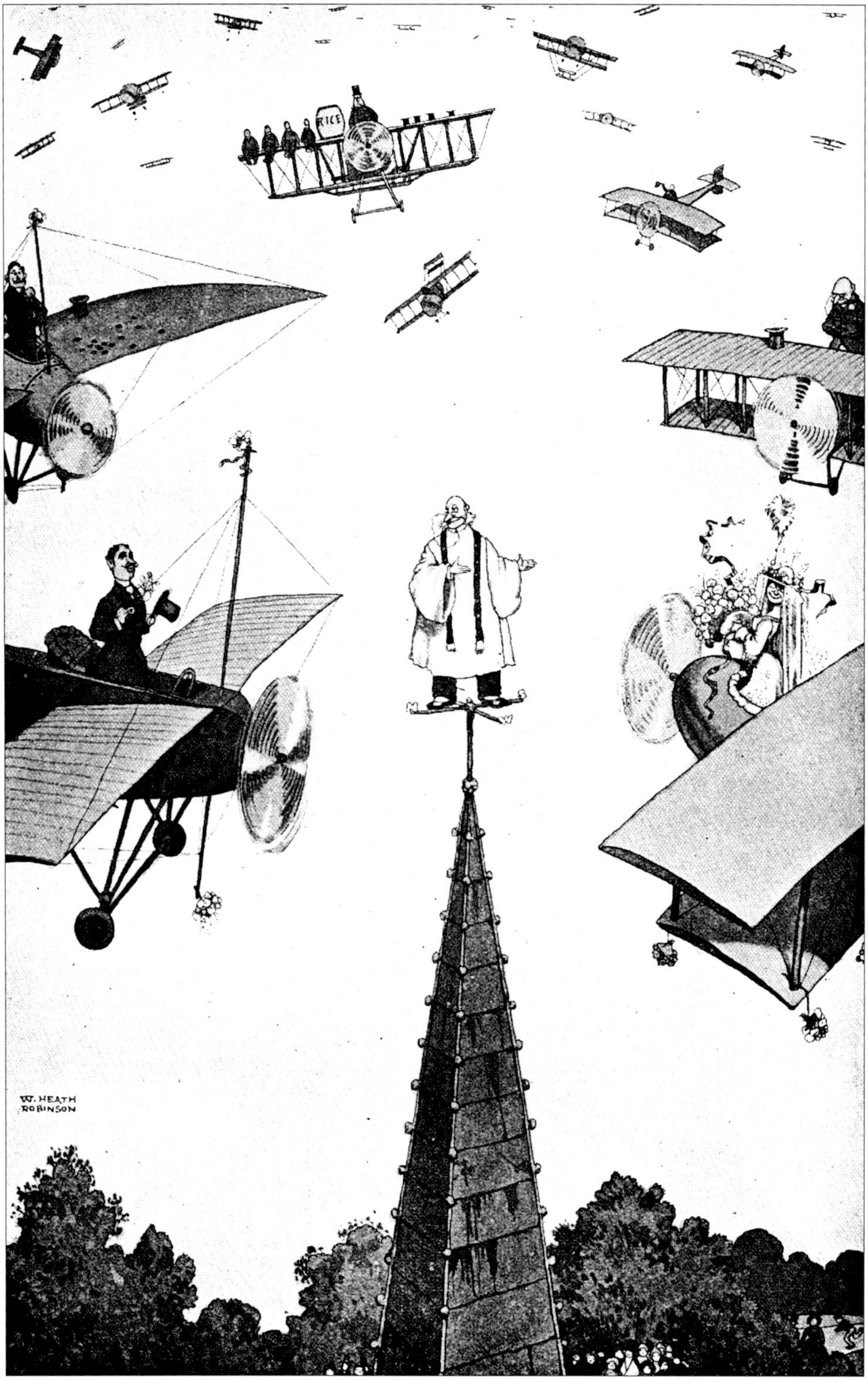
RICE
W. HEATH ROBINSON

The first aero wedding.

EVENING SOLACE

ILLUSION

ILLUSION
CAUSED BY
TWO PLANES
PASSING THROUGH
A CLOUD

WHERE THE INVENTOR OF THE PROPELLER FIRST GOT THE IDEA

ANOTHER
CURIOUS
ILLUSION

Silhouettes (3).

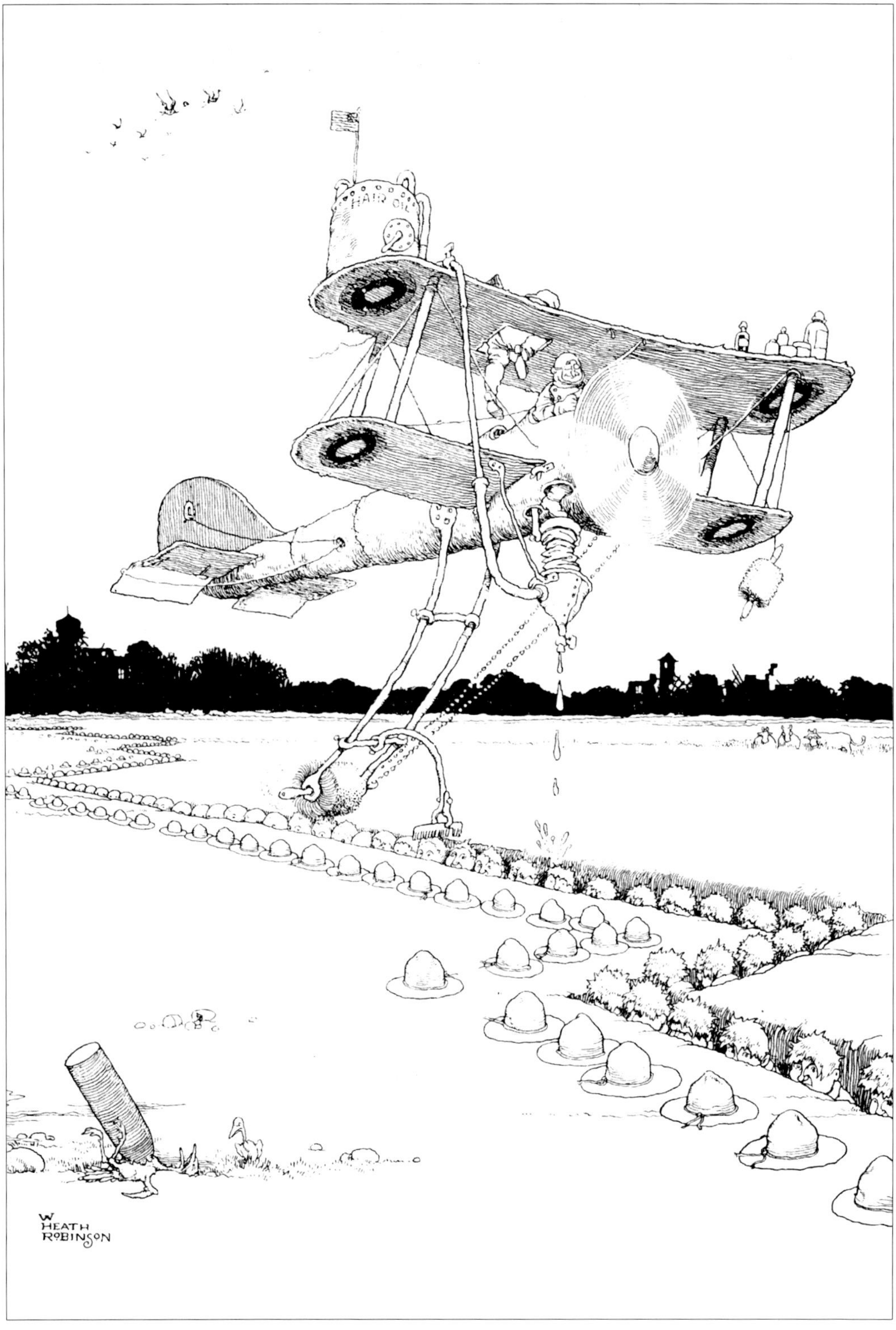
HAIR OIL
W HEATH ROBINSON

The Haroplane.

Petty aero larceny I: Stealing a dinner.

Petty aero larceny II: Pinching laundry.

Heroic rescue from a falling tower.

The water coupe: an elegant little car for the convenience of anglers.

A leak in the Channel Tunnel.

A time saver for the plane business man: how aviation enables the busy city man to get a sea dip between business appointments.

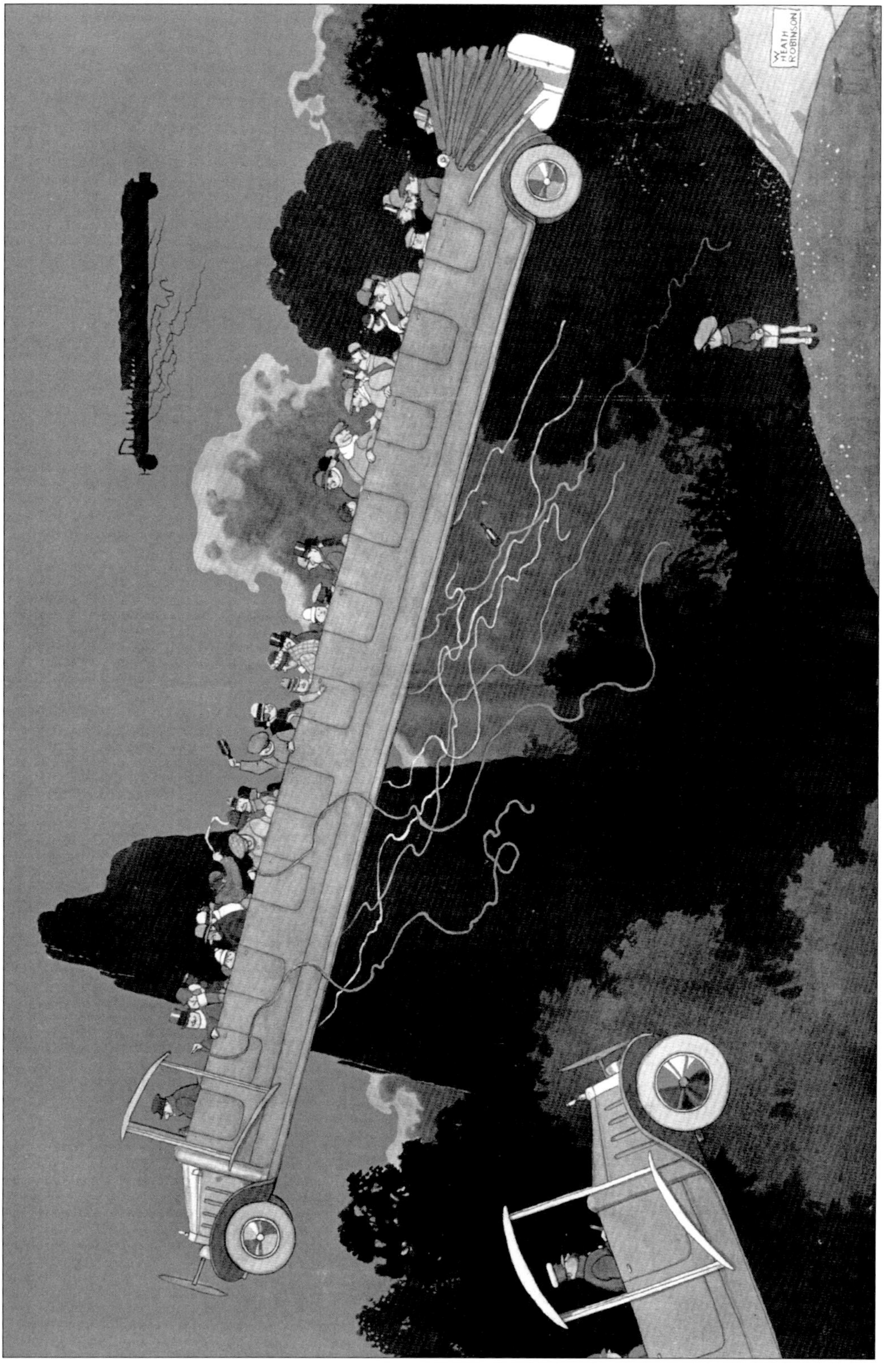
W. HEATH ROBINSON

The Aerocharrybang.

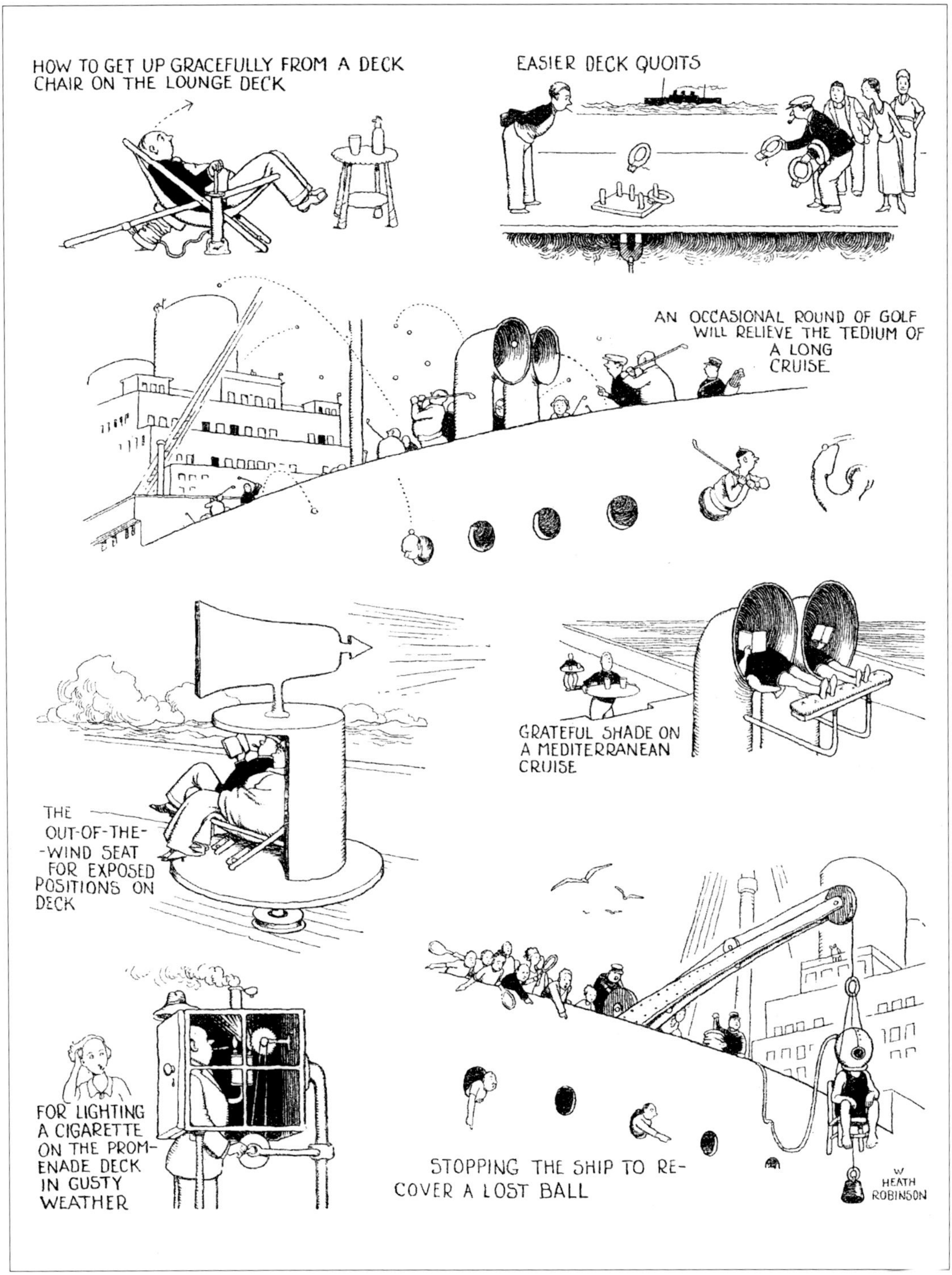
HOW TO GET UP GRACEFULLY FROM A DECK CHAIR ON THE LOUNGE DECK
EASIER DECK QUOITS
AN OCCASIONAL ROUND OF GOLF WILL RELIEVE THE TEDIUM OF A LONG CRUISE
GRATEFUL SHADE ON A MEDITERRANEAN CRUISE
THE OUT-OF-THE-WIND SEAT FOR EXPOSED POSITIONS ON DECK
FOR LIGHTING A CIGARETTE ON THE PROMENADE DECK IN GUSTY WEATHER
STOPPING THE SHIP TO RECOVER A LOST BALL
W HEATH ROBINSON

The summer cruise.

How is the ship's anchor weighed?

The 'write' of way. Love at first sight.

The subzeppmarinellin.

Before the advent of GWR turbine steamers on the Fishguard–Rosslare route to Ireland.

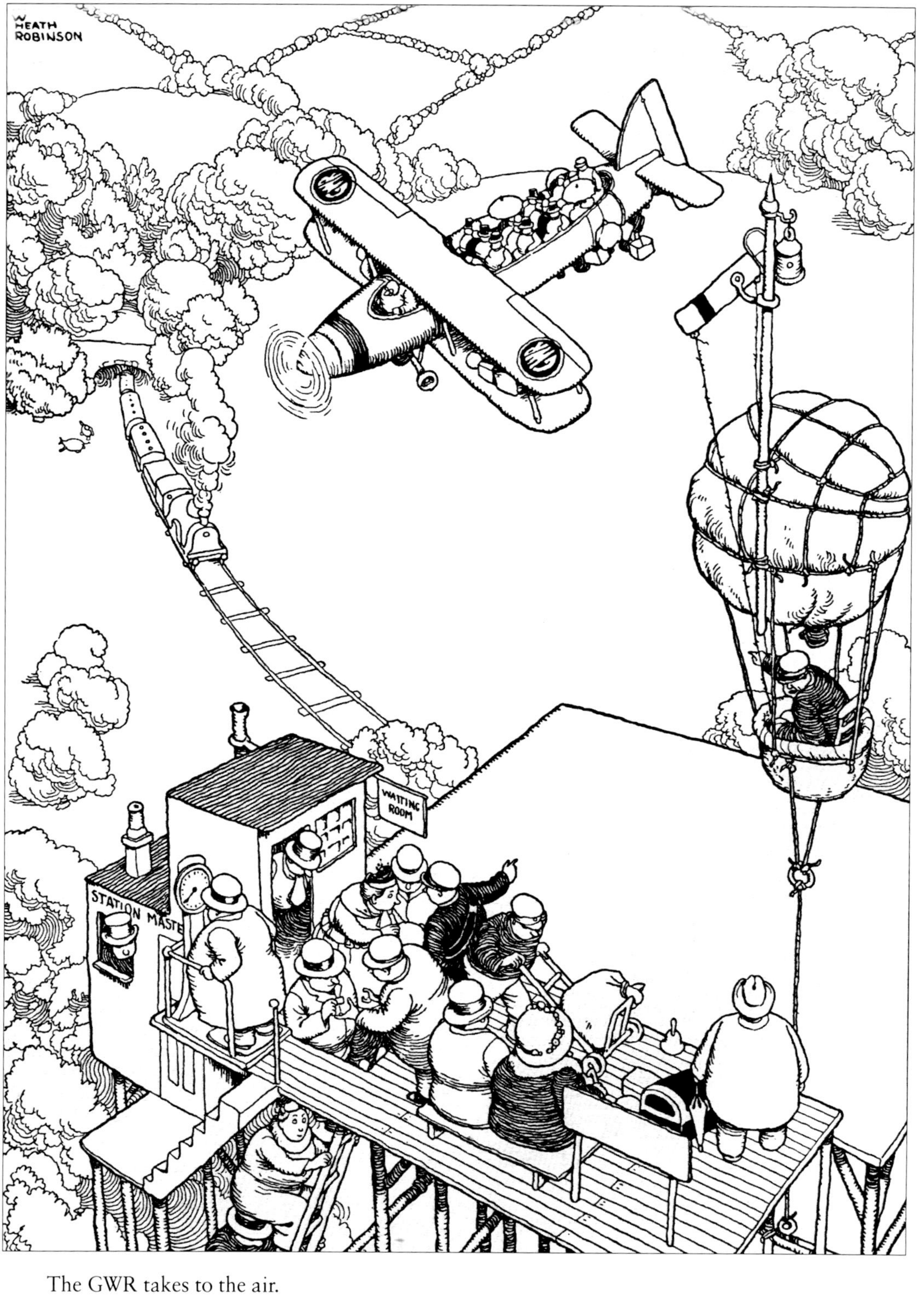
W HEATH ROBINSON
WAITING ROOM
STATION MASTE

The GWR takes to the air.

Safety first: the winner of the first prize offered by *The Bystander* for the best home made safety glider.

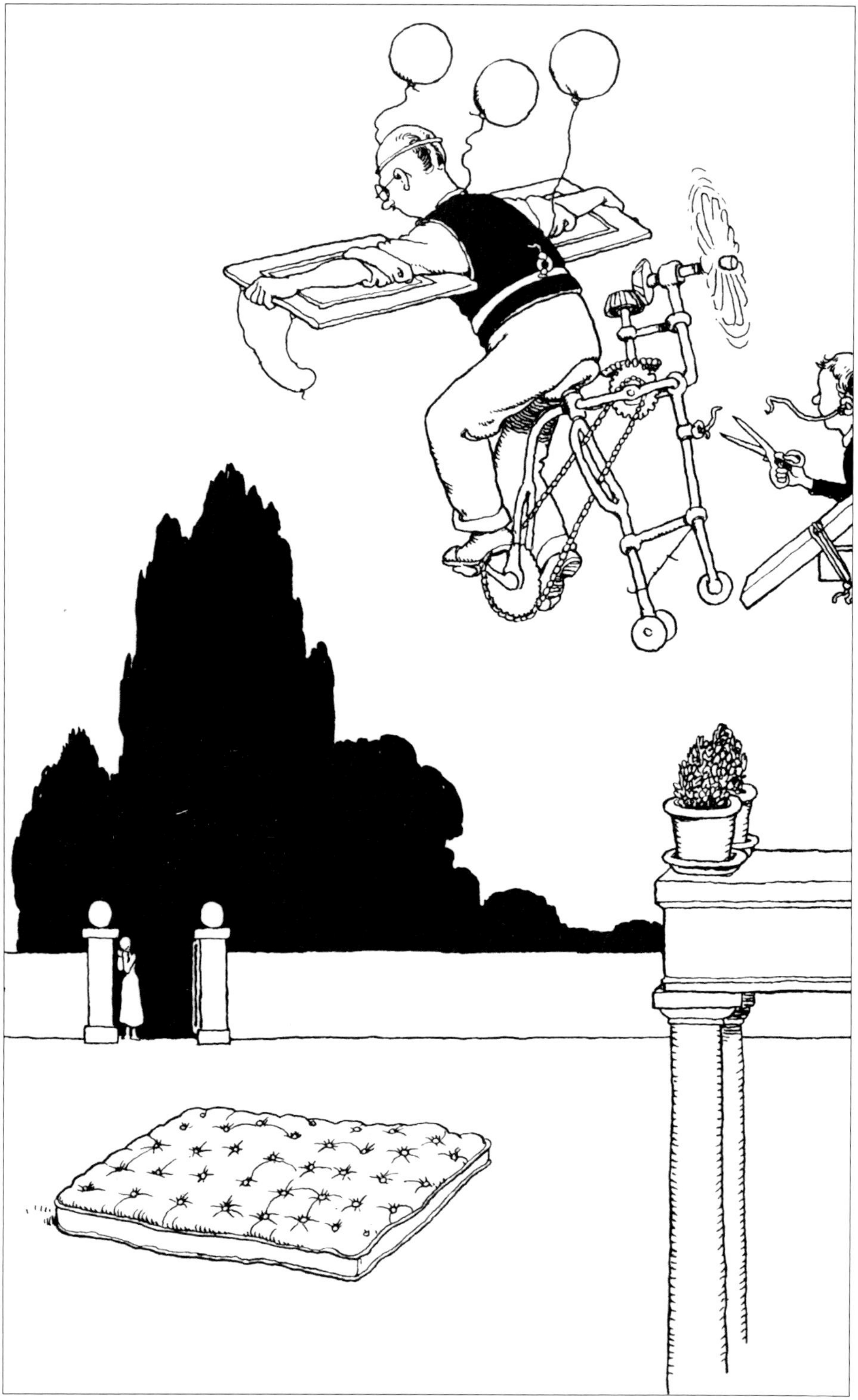

The aero-widow.

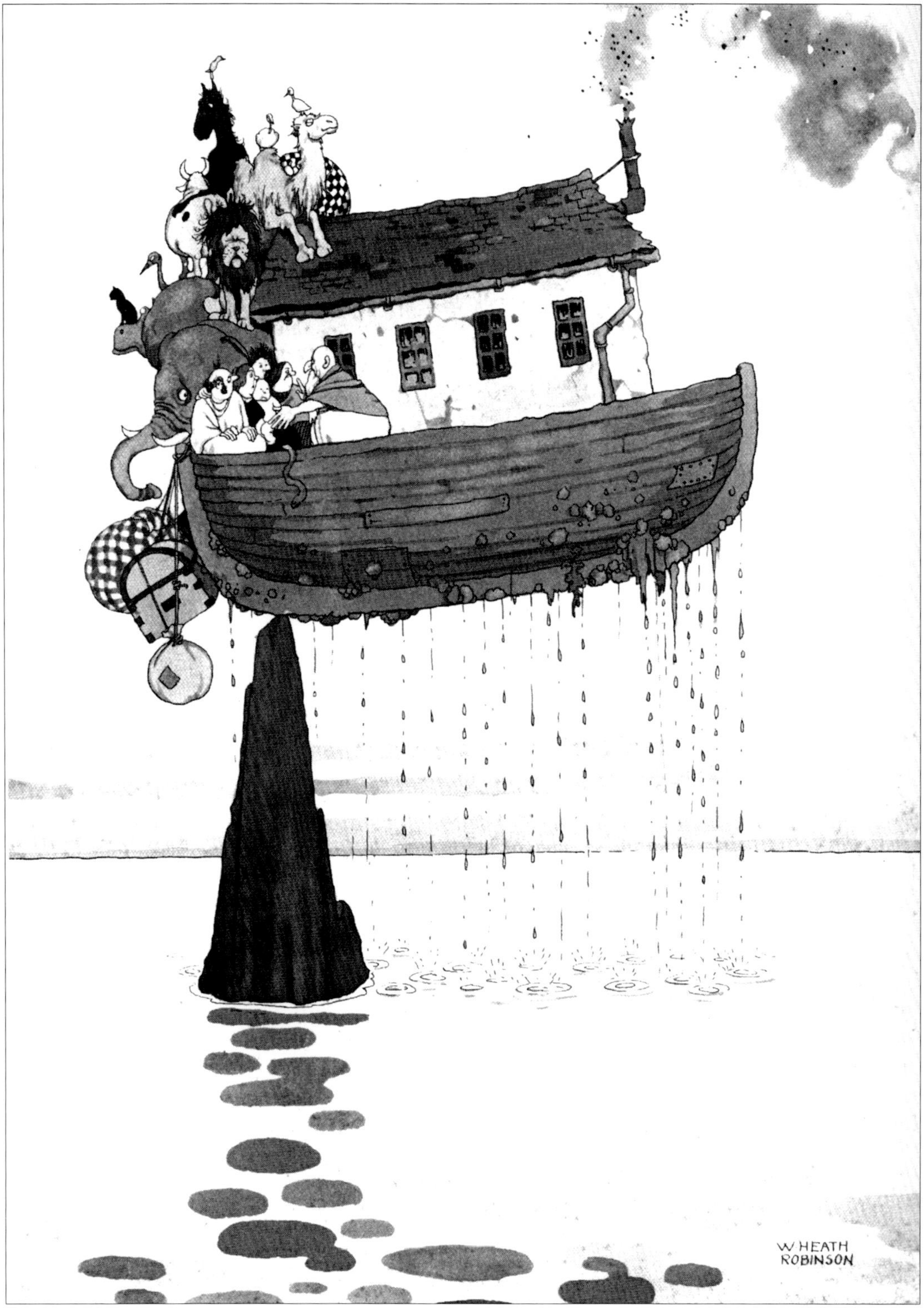
W HEATH
ROBINSON

Noah and the flood.

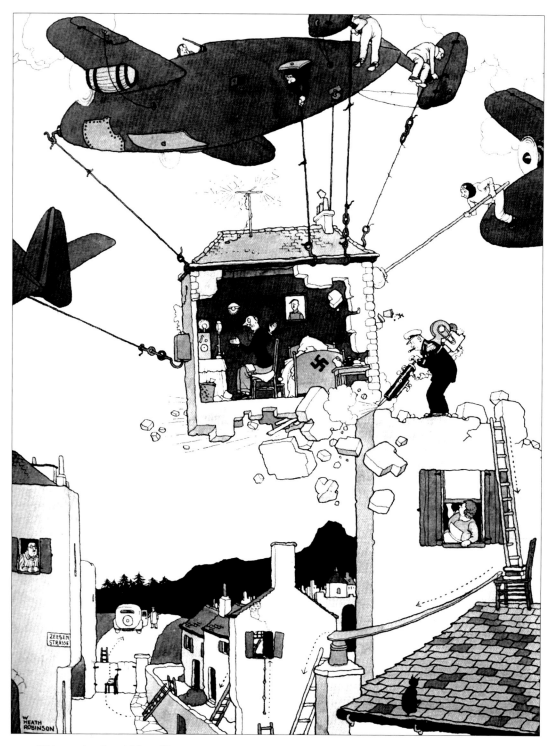

Kidnapping Lord Haw-Haw.

Christmas family gliders.

The new holiday aeroplane.

Swimming the Channel: some simple devices to ensure success.